Harriet Tubman
A Lesson in Bravery

Elizabeth Kernan

The Rosen Publishing Group, Inc.
New York

Published in 2002 by The Rosen Publishing Group, Inc.
29 East 21st Street, New York, NY 10010

Book Design: Haley Wilson

Photo Credits: Cover, p. 1 © SuperStock; pp. 5, 6, 9, 11, 13, 15, 17, 18, 21 © Corbis-Bettmann.

ISBN: 0-8239-8229-7
6-pack ISBN: 0-8239-8632-2

Manufactured in the United States of America

Contents

Born into Slavery

Araminta Ross, also known by her mother's name, Harriet, was born into **slavery** on a Maryland **plantation** in 1820. She lived during a terrible time when many people in the United States owned slaves. Slaves were brought over from Africa and forced to work on plantations. The **master** or slave owner bought and sold slaves and told them what to do. Some slaves escaped to the northern United States where many African Americans were free.

Slaves worked long hours picking cotton in the fields or doing housework without pay.

6

Harriet's Childhood

Slaves lived in small **shacks** with no windows and little furniture. Slaves worked either in the fields or in the houses of the slave owners. At the age of five, Harriet was sent to do housework for a woman in another home. Harriet was beaten whenever the **mistress** was unhappy with her work.

Many slaves lived in small shacks with no windows.

Hard Times

A slave owner once became so angry at Harriet for not helping him catch a runaway slave that he threw a heavy object that hit her on the head. The object hurt Harriet's brain and she almost died. For the rest of her life, Harriet suffered from fainting spells and dizziness.

Harriet faced many difficult times during the years she lived as a slave.

9

Dreams of Freedom

Harriet heard stories about many slaves who wanted their **freedom**. She knew that some slaves had fought back against their masters and escaped to the northern United States. She married John Tubman, a freed slave, in 1844. Harriet was afraid that she would be sold and separated from John. She began to plan her escape.

Many slaves lived in shacks on a plantation like this one in Georgia.

11

The Underground Railroad

Harriet heard of slaves who chose to escape slavery on the "Underground Railroad." The Underground Railroad was not underground and it was not a railroad. It was a secret trail that runaway slaves followed from the South through the North, and sometimes into Canada. Harriet decided to escape on the Underground Railroad.

Many slaves risked their lives for freedom. Some slaves hid in wooden boxes and were put on trains heading North.

Escape to Freedom

Many brave people risked their lives to help Harriet and other slaves escape. Some people gave them directions, food, and a place to sleep during their trip through the Underground Railroad. Harriet sometimes traveled in a wagon and other times in a boat. She walked through forests at night and hid in barns during the day.

More than 100,000 slaves escaped to freedom with the help of people who ran the Underground Railroad.

15

Finally Free

Harriet arrived in Philadelphia, Pennsylvania, in 1849. After thirty years of living as a slave, Harriet finally had her freedom! She worried about the family and friends she had left behind in the South. Harriet decided to return to the South to help them gain their freedom.

Like Harriet, many slaves escaped through the Underground Railroad.

18

Helping Other Slaves

Harriet found a job working in a kitchen in Philadelphia. She used the money she made to travel back and forth to the South. Working as a **conductor**, Harriet helped slaves escape through the Underground Railroad. A conductor used wagons with false bottoms to help slaves travel from one **station** to another. These were homes where slaves stopped for food, rest, and a change of clothes.

Harriet (far left) helped this family and many others escape to the North.

Harriet's Bravery

Harriet spent eleven years working to free more than 300 slaves through the Underground Railroad. She faced the danger of getting **captured** every time she returned to the South. Harriet continued to **rescue** slaves even after slave owners offered $40,000 for her capture.

Harriet traveled to the South nineteen times to rescue slaves.

21

Fighting for a Cause

Harriet made her last trip to the South in 1860. Later she served as a nurse, a spy, and a **scout** for the Union army in the North during the Civil War. She continued to fight for other causes throughout her life, such as women's rights and education for African Americans. She lived to be ninety-three years old.

Glossary

capture   To make a prisoner of someone.

conductor   A person who worked on the Underground Railroad and helped to free slaves.

freedom   The power to do, say, or think as you please.

master   A slave owner who has authority over slaves on a plantation.

mistress   The wife of a master or the lady of the plantation who had authority over slaves.

plantation   A large farm where cotton, tobacco, or sugarcane was grown by people who lived there.

rescue   To save someone from danger or harm.

scout   Someone sent to find out what the enemy is doing.

shack   A roughly built hut or little house.

slavery   The system of one person "owning" another.

station   A place where slaves stopped to receive directions, food, clothing, and help when escaping to the North.

Index